Girl, YOU ARE A WARRIOR

A BATTLE PLAN TO RECLAIM YOUR VOICE, YOUR VALUE, AND YOUR PURPOSE

AYANA HENDERSON

Book Design by Allison Denise of Brand It Beautifully

ISBN: 978-1-7374212-0-7

Printed in the United States of America

Dedication

I dedicate this book to:

To my mom who has supported me at every step of the
way. A woman who would never let me forget my value,
especially in the moments I struggled so much to see it
myself. For your guidance and strength as a woman, a
mother and a wife. You are my very first example of a
Warrior. I love you and miss you. I hope I've made you
proud.

Table of Contents

She believed she could

So she did.

Introduction

Welcome to warrior womanhood and thank you for purchasing this book. My hope is that by the time you reach the end of this book you will have made the decision to walk in self-acceptance and self-love.

If you are reading this book, then I know you are ready to break free from operating in performance-based love and living up to the expectations others have placed on you, but you are in need of a process and real action steps that can get you to the woman within you who's ready to break free.

You have found yourself trapped in the spirit of comparison and looking at all the picture-perfect women, moms, and wives on Instagram who are posting their perfect lives or are on Facebook sharing all their inspiring posts of overcoming circumstances and trials. Yeah, I know that struggle well. Something inside you says, *Why can't my life look like that?* You likely are exhausted from all the people-pleasing or of always trying to be "the supermom," "the submissive wife," and the "Proverbs 31 woman." Trying to live up to all the expectations of all these roles is suffocating you. What happens when you suffocate from this pressure? It's hard to breathe and you die. How can you continue to breathe life into others when you are out of breath yourself? However, you try. Your faith is at best luke-warm, and you are wondering where God is in all this. How could He just leave you like this? Why do you feel this way? Through it all, you still have hope. You hope that you can feel like YOU again, but you need a starting point; you need a resource that won't just leave you inspired but give you tangible tools to put into practice in your life.

All you want is to feel like YOU again. Deep down, you know you are more than what your life looks like right now. You can see a better version of your life for you, your kids, and your marriage. I can see that for you too! You have everything it takes, right in this moment, as you are to start making that change.

I remember asking myself, *Where has the woman who was fierce and full of life gone? The one who spoke up and spoke out? Where did she go?* I looked up one day, and I was Javon's mom, Sekai's mom, Anaya's mom, and Levi's mom. I also was Charles's wife, and prior to that, I typically was identified as Otto's daughter. Even at work, I was called "HR" most of the time. Slowly but surely, I would perform differently when I served in each of these roles. That's seven different roles, which represented seven different versions of me. It was exhausting.

After hitting a low point in my life, I realized I had to become a mature woman before I could function properly in any of my assigned roles. I had to strip away all the titles and ask myself, *Who am I without all of that?*

I knew I had value. I knew I could be doing more with my life. I didn't know I could fix it until God showed me that I could! He showed me three key things along my healing journey: my identity in Christ, self-acceptance, and self-love.

I began to understand God's love for me as His child and as a woman from a Biblical perspective. He showed me how He designed women to be. He wanted to show me that we were not weak, but rather He designed us to be Warriors. That I had everything in me to become the woman I desired to be.

Not only has this healing journey changed the trajectory of my life, but the effects of it are generational. My children won't have to deal with extreme anger, suicidal thoughts, rage, resentment, bitterness, and the list goes on because I'm dealing with it myself, and they are watching me. Their children will be free because I will have freed their parents. You see, it was so much bigger than me.

Having gone through the journey I am about to share with you in the pages ahead, I now walk in the full authority of who God has called me to be as a woman, not as a mom or a wife, but as a woman. My voice is stronger, louder, and more confident. My value and my worth are solidified in Christ and not in the world, and I could not be convinced that my purpose is not what it is today. Each step of the process and the journey has made an imprint on my heart. I've sat in board rooms with millionaires, held high titles with an associate's degree, encouraged mothers and wives and equipped them with practical tools, helped women find and own their authentic voice, and became a wife who has a Biblical impact on her husband.

This book provides you with real-life situations, applicable and practical steps and useful tools, and tips toward becoming the woman you and God desires you to be. Your personal battle plan, which includes the tools needed for your battle kit. In each chapter, you will have an opportunity to "dig" a little deeper with reflection questions and prayer. The questions are designed to pull out what's not working and expose what can be changed. You have the control and the abilityWork at your pace but do the work. You will thank yourself for it.

By the end of the book, you will be on a path to reclaiming your voice, your value, and your purpose all with a battle kit in hand. It's time to release the Warrior within. Are you ready?

CHAPTER 1

I Prayed for This?

I NEVER THOUGHT MY LIFE would mimic something right out of a Madea movie. My life was the story in which a woman who looks to have it all. She has a good, nice home and is well taken care of. Then, her relationship takes a turn for the worse, and she is left down and out and completely depleted. As she tries to pick up the pieces of her life, her Prince Charming comes along, and while they go through some initial struggles, she realizes that he is exactly what she needs, and they live happily ever after. Yeah, that is my story. I know it well.

I remember when I ended my first marriage, I thought nobody was going to want a woman who had four children, especially two of her children at a very young age.

My daughter was just shy of two years old, and my youngest son wasn't even one year old. I thought, *Nobody's going to want to be in a relationship with a woman with all these kids.* This wasn't back in the old days when women were popping out 7, 8, 9 children. Having more than two kids at that time was considered to be taboo, and here I was with 4 children. The assumption that I was a whore or that I could have 4 different baby daddies, which wasn't the case, hit me like bricks. Constantly having to defend my childbearing choices while on dates was enough to make me just want to be single. I remember praying and asking God to send me a man who would accept me and my children. I asked God that the man would not be into street life and would not drink or smoke. I wanted a man who knew God, was responsible, and could carry a conversation. I needed a man who didn't come with baby mama drama and wanted things for his life that he was working actively to achieve.

Despite the prayer that I prayed, I still felt like no man was going to want to deal with all this because it was just so much. Those feelings changed when I met my current husband. At that time in my life, I was a pastry chef running a successful home-based cake decorating business. As a single woman, Valentine's Day was a bit of a drag, so every February, I would host Sweets for My Sweets. It was an event that was designed for both singles and couples as well as other home-based bakers and local eateries. The vendors would provide bite-sized treats and samples for the guests as a way to gain business and didn't make singles feel awkward about celebrating this day. Couples could enjoy a nice, no-pressure evening of music, food, and fun.

My current husband said he received a social media invite from a mutual friend. While at the event, he shared a review on Yelp, and Yelp retweeted his review. We ended up connecting on social media a few days later. About a week or two later, I put out a post on Facebook saying that I had mini-sized banana pudding leftovers, and anybody who wanted a small banana pudding could purchase one. Quite a few people responded, and he was one of them. He came later that night to pick up his order, and we sat and talked for maybe about 2 to 2 1/2 hours. We still don't know what prompted such a long conversation over a $10 banana pudding, but I found him to be very intriguing and safe. He shared how he was also in a similar situation, so he could relate to a lot of what I was experiencing. The interesting thing that happened was all my kids gravitated to him. At one point, my daughter, who was just under two years old, started climbing all over him, and he just went along with it and entertained her. He didn't seem bothered or overwhelmed with my children. The conversation came to an end, and he went home. We didn't talk much over the next few months, but we remained friends on social media.

Then, just before the summer hit, I moved into a new apartment. What I didn't know was that I happened to move right across the street from him. One morning, about a week after I moved in, he sent me a message through Facebook saying, " Hey I think your car is on the street!" I told him most people see my car on the street! I had my cake business decals all over my car, so customers often honked their horns or flagged me down, and new clients would take a picture and order later. I asked him when he saw my car, and he told me he was looking right at it. I thought that was weird because I was at home. I told him I was at home at that moment. He said, "I think it's on my street then!" I asked what street he lived on, and he said the same street name! I shared that we just moved into #17, and he told me that he lived at #14.

About a month after moving in, he and I gradually got to know each other. We would hang out with each other, sitting outside on my front steps talking about anything and everything. My kids gradually got to know him too. We were both dating here and there, but we were not dating each other. Our daily talks turned into walks, and that continued for the next year and a half.

In the Spring of that following year, a mutual friend asked a group of us to come out and support a friend of his who was playing piano for a jazz band at the Top of the Hub in Boston. It was an upscale restaurant that overlooked the entire city and was on the 52nd floor of the Prudential Center. It had the best steak! Unfortunately, it's closed now, but man, it was a sight to see. As we were getting ready separately, we kept sending each other picture messages of the outfits we were trying on. We weren't quite sure if this was a date or not, and we later realized that we both asked ourselves if this was a date. We ended up referring to that weekend as our "This is a date. I don't know if this is a date. This might be a *real* date."

After we left the restaurant, we went to a nightclub where his friend was celebrating the release of her book, and we danced the night away well until 2:00a.m. When that ended, we just drove around the city for a little bit and ended up just outside Boston Logan Airport. I have a thing for airplanes. I love watching them take off and land, and I wonder where they are coming from or where they are going. I could sit and watch them all day. We found a spot and parked, and for the next couple of hours, we talked and watched planes fly right over our heads. We were out until maybe about 4:00-5:00a.m.. I think at that point we kind of knew we were starting to like each other but didn't really entertain it. About a month later, we decided that maybe we would like to date, but being a man of God, he wanted to go about it the right way. I had just ended a relationship with a man I was dating in April, and here I was, a month later, wanting to date this guy. However, he wasn't just a random guy. He was someone who over that last year and a half took the time to get to know me, inside and out. He showed me what prayer looked like. He talked to me about God. We explored the city together on our long walks. We cried together and encouraged each other. When I found out I was diabetic, he signed us up for a gym membership, and we worked out 3x a week until I was able to get my numbers under control. He wasn't just some guy. He had become my best friend. Then, he talked to my kids about it, and they liked the idea. We hadn't made anything official, but we were kind of a thing. Over the next few weeks, our conversations transitioned to if I would want more kids and how we both felt about getting married again. I really didn't think much of it beyond the general conversation. I think we wanted to know if we wanted the same things and were on the same page. We would talk about those things, and I would just think, *At some point, we may get married, but right now, we are just dating.* Y'all know how us girls can be! We get all excited and start planning the wedding from day 1. I knew he was different. I knew I needed to heal. I knew I was open to marriage and love again. I just didn't know when those things would happen. He did send me a few rings, so he could get my opinion, but I had no idea what was really happening.

Then, on the 4th of July, we decided we were going to do the traditional cookout hopping. We would start at my family's house. Then, we would head to his dad's house just south of Boston. We hadn't met each other's family yet, so this was our first real introduction to each other's families. My dad had been in a rehab facility after having surgery, so we agreed to pick him up. When we arrived, we all went in, so the kids could say a proper hello, and I could introduce him to my dad. He asked if he could speak to my dad, so I gathered my dad's belongings for the day and took them and the kids to the car. What I thought was my dad giving him "the talk" was really him asking for my hand in marriage. Earlier that day, I saw that he and my mom were talking while I was getting the kids ready for the cookouts. What I didn't know was he also was asking my mom and my two older boys for my hand as well. He had shown all of them the ring. The only request that my son made was that he would do it when they could be there. My son was about to head to California to spend time with my brother, and he wanted to be there. After a long day between the two cookouts, we headed back to his dad's house to end the day. Right there, under the fireworks, he proposed. Five and a half weeks later, we were married.

When I say I was the Madea story, I was the woman who was down and out trying to pick up the pieces of her life, and this man came along, and he was everything that she thought she couldn't have. He showed her what was possible, and they went on living their happily ever after.

With life, there are many moments that are valley lows and mountaintop highs. What I didn't know was how necessary the valleys were. I did not realize how many lessons I would learn, and I did not realize that things would stretch and grow me in ways I hadn't imagined. What really hit me about being in the valley was the only way to get what I prayed for was to grow through what I needed. Even in the valley, God will give you hope, but you're still in the Valley. For a long time, I felt like I was in the valley with my first marriage, and then, I hit a point in my current marriage and remember thinking, *God, how many times will I have to be in the valley?* I prayed for this, and I wasn't even fully in Christ yet, but sometimes what you pray to receive comes with lessons you didn't plan to learn.

When we got remarried, some people were happy and joyful for us, and some people were apprehensive and critical of us. Some of our friends and family were on the fence because after all, we still hadn't met most of each other's family. Additionally, the period during which we dated and got engaged was a total of 15.5 weeks. They didn't care that we had known each other for almost 2 years prior to our marriage. To them, our marriage was sudden. Our wedding would be the first time that they met each other. Some people came to the ceremony late, some people did not come at all. One person even walked down my aisle as we were in the middle of our ceremony. We focused on who was there that day including those who loved us and wanted to be a genuine support to our union.

Many of my family members saw the Madea movie play out too. To them, my story looked as if I went from a bad marriage that left me broken to now owning a home in a nice neighborhood. My kids were going to better schools. We had two cars in the driveway and had a manicured lawn. We also were able to host family events.

From the outside looking in, everything looked so picture-perfect, but it's something about being able to look at someone's house from the outside without peeping in the window to really see what actually is going on on the inside. There were a lot of things happening on the inside.

Internally, I was struggling to be a good mom, a submissive wife, and a Proverbs 31 woman. I really couldn't see the blessings that some of my family members once saw. Had I become that ungrateful? Was I blind? Why was there such a disconnect between what others saw and what I felt? Where was the disconnect? I'm just thinking, *You guys have no idea how I feel!* It made my skin crawl at every compliment. I wanted to feel what they felt and see what they saw, and I couldn't quite reconcile it all. There I was. I was back in the valley.

When you pray, be mindful that not only can God bless you with what you prayed to receive, but He'll also give you what you need. Sometimes, those are the lessons in the things that you didn't plan to occur. There was a lot of maturing and a lot of growing that I needed to do, especially as someone new in Christ.

How did my valley look? My valley looked like my prayer was answered, but it all came with a lot of struggles. I lost my voice, the ability to see my value, my spunk, and my hope because I had operated so long with limiting beliefs. My valley exposed my many shortcomings as a mother. My valley left me feeling unseen, unloved, devalued, hopeless, and rejected. I was a worrier, and I was wounded. However, the biggest part of being in the valley was that I was the common denominator. This valley was mine and mine alone.

God began to show me how I was having character complications in my marriage. I don't know if struggling is the right word, but my marriage was struggling. My kids were starting to give me feedback about performance as a mom, and my husband gave me feedback about my performance as a wife. It was just a lot to handle and go through. I didn't even know how the healing or reconciliation processes would look. I was losing hope, and I was tired of being in the valley.

Let's Dig:

You don't automatically just go from the valley to the mountaintop. There are lessons in the journey as you climb to the mountaintop. It is those lessons that you will need to be able to experience the fullness of what God has for you. Even when I walk through the darkest valley, I will not be afraid, for you are close beside me. Your rod and your staff protect and comfort me. (Psalm 23:4, NIV). Even in the valley, there's hope but it's still the valley. Glean what you can during those moments because they do prepare you for the next stage.

Father God, I pray for the sister reading this right now. As she reads this chapter, there may be some things that creep in her spirit. There may be things you wanted her to see or expose to her. There may be things with which she has connected. Maybe, she too feels like she is in the valley. I pray that you comfort her the way you comforted me. Sit her on your lap as the Good Father that you are and show her the way. Remind her of your love for her and that even though she may be in the valley, it's there where she will begin to feel and experience your love for her even though she is flawed and all. Have your way in her heart and love her through and through. In Jesus Name, I pray.

Take a moment to search your own heart.

Are you experiencing a valley moment in your life?

What are some ways in which people's perception of you doesn't match how you perceive yourself?

List the disconnects. Take a piece of paper and draw a line down the middle. On one side write what others have observed and shared to you about your life - label this side EXTERNAL. *For example, people thought I was living a good life.* On the other side, write down the truth of what you really feel - label this INTERNAL. *For example, the truth was I was broken, depressed, angry and felt alone.*

After completing this list, the one thing I want you to realize is that you are in control of the internal - the "you" in this. You are in control of your thoughts, feelings, beliefs and actions. You can do something about and change all that you listed. In the next chapter, we will talk about how feedback is a crucial part of the process.

CHAPTER 2

The Experience of You

"Human anger does not produce the righteousness God desires."
– (James 1:20, NLT)

You NEVER KNOW THE fullness of who you are until someone else shares their experiences of you.

Back in the summer of 2016, my two sons, ages 16 and 11 at the time, were headed to visit my brother and his family in California. It was about two or three in the morning. They were flying alone at the time. We went up to the ticket booth to get their tickets. The agent gave us the OK, gave us their passes, and directed us to the gate, so we could walk them to their terminal because they were unaccompanied minors. My oldest son was 16, and my younger son was probably about 11.

I wanted to make sure that they got on the plane with no problems. We headed to the security checkpoint, so we could go through it, and were told, "It's one adult per child." My husband and I were there with the two boys, so we figured that we could go back with them because each of us could go with one of our sons. Expecting that we could back with them, we were ready to proceed. We explained that they were brothers, but the TSA agent then decided that only one parent could go with them. I felt my blood starting to boil. He also said that I would need to return to the ticket counter to get a "parent pass" in order to escort them to their gate.

I went back to the ticket counter and shared what the TSA agent said. The ticketing agent responded by saying, "I don't know why they would say that. You have the unaccompanied minor forms. Their minors. Why do you need the pass?" I went back and I explained to him what the agent said, and he sent me back to the ticket counter. I had to go through this back and forth process maybe two or three times.

At this point, my head was starting to hurt. Panic settled in because I realized they may now miss their flight with all this foolishness. I was tired, and I just wanted to get them on the plane and go home because I had to be at work in a couple of hours. My annoyance and anger was starting to come full throttle.

Finally, I got the ticket that I needed. My anger and frustration was apparent. Then, I heard the words, "Calm down," and I lost it. In all the history of "calm downs" hardly anyone has ever calmed down! At that point, I was yelling at the TSA agent because he was wasting time. In my mind, I needed to get my kids to the other side of the airport, so they could make their flight to California. After about 10-15 minutes of making a whole entire scene in the airport, cussing, carrying on, and hand clapping (I mean, a scene straight out of Love and Hip Hop), I got them to the gate. I asked them to text me to let me know that they were taking off and text me again when the plane landed.

As my husband and I were driving back home, I got an additional text from my oldest son. He asked me if I could do him a favor. I was thinking, *"Maybe, he forgot something or maybe, he left something on the plane. Maybe, he wants me to remember to do something for him.* It was none of those. He said, "Mom, I need you to work on your anger. It's embarrassing." My heart sank. It felt like I couldn't breathe. I felt instantly embarrassed and ashamed. All I could say was "OK." I didn't ask him what he meant. I just said "OK."

The level of shame and guilt that I felt in that moment was tremendous because I realized that I had brought on my own child shame and embarrassment. I didn't even know what to do with myself. I didn't even realize I was this bad. I was so consumed in my anger, my rage, and my bitterness that I didn't even know I was dealing with those things. I didn't even know what was causing my anger, but I now knew it was coming out. It was starting to affect my family; it was starting to affect my relationships. Mostly, it was affecting me and how I showed up in the world. I didn't know how I was going to fix it, but I committed from that moment forward to work on my anger actively.

There is something about asking for help or receiving feedback that helps you to see your blind spots when you're receptive to it.

I have always been the mom who has checked in with my kids and allowed them the space to be able to provide me with feedback in a respectable way and without consequence. My oldest son used to write me notes and leave them on my bed. They mostly focused on how he thought about me as a mom and how he saw our relationship. Here is a one note that he wrote me when he was 11 years old:

"Dear Mom,

I feel like you don't love me anymore. I feel like you spend more time with your other kids than you spend with me. You don't care about me.

Your son."

At the time he wrote that, I had just had child number three and had just found out I was pregnant with child number four. He was overwhelmed with children, and so was I. He had me all to himself for 4 1/2 years. When his brother came along, things were still manageable. However, by the time there were three children in the home with one more coming he was too overwhelmed with the thought of sharing me with anyone else. His sister was a handful. Full of energy and a little busy body, very different from he and his brother's laid back personalities. He expressed his feelings with me in his way, through letters. We sometimes forget as parents that our decision has an effect on our children's mental and emotional health as well.

I received feedback from not only my kids but also my family members, friends, co-workers, and supervisors. Even in arguments with my loved ones, things came out about my character that I didn't know, didn't want to accept, and didn't want to believe were true about me, but they were true.

Sometimes, we disregard this information because we think people are expressing themselves in the heat of the moment. We think, *They're angry. They just said that to hurt me. There is no truth to what they said.*

However, every time I've taken a step back, I have recognized that there's always *some* truth to it. It could be 100% true, or it could be 10% true, but usually, there's *some* truth to it. Either you're coming across in such a way or the way you're behaving is so consistent (good or bad) that they see patterns that you just don't see.

I've always recognized that even in those moments when you're having heated debates, discussions, and differences of opinion, those things can come up and start to show you some more about your character.

I remember having a conversation with my second son about a year later after this airport incident. He's now about 12 or 13 years old. We were in the kitchen, and we we're talking about basketball. I asked him what were some things he liked about his new school, and I asked him about his interest in signing up for a basketball program. We talked about his commitment to basketball. When he was about 9 years old, I had signed him up for football, but when he was playing, he decided after the first day that he couldn't do it because he knew that if he hit and hurt another kid, that reality would bother him, and he didn't want another kid to get hurt. We continued talking, and I started asking him questions around what else might he be interested in doing or what else was going on at his new school. He kept responding with the shoulder shrug, the quick "yes," and no answers at all. I asked him why he kept answering me with one or two words. Very nonchalantly, he said, "You don't care about any of the things that I care about." My heart sank once again. Once again, one of my kids was telling me about me and my relationship with him. As a mom, you hear that, and you think, "I absolutely DO care about the things that you care about!"

I had been so caught up in challenges that were happening in my marriage, work, and life that trying to balance four kids at home and being a new person in Christ blinded me to the fact that I was completely neglecting my kids emotionally. My kids felt very unseen. I didn't even recognize that I appeared to be disinterested in things that interested him.

"Control your anger, for anger labels you a fool."
– (Ecclesiastes 7:9, NLT)

He was right. I wasn't showing that I cared even though I did care. I just lost sight of how I was showing up as a mom. I committed, once again, to make sure that I was showing interest and not just showing up on the surface. I needed to show up and cheer and celebrate the big and small wins. I needed to look for opportunities to engage in conversation actively, encourage him in moments of challenge, and become interested in even the small things that were important to him like the style of basketball sneakers that he liked and the reason he wanted to join this team. I committed to be at the practices and talk to the coaches and really show him that not only did I care but also I wanted to be involved and committed to his growth as a basketball player. I wanted to show him that I wanted to commit to his growth as a person, and sit down and have those conversations with him.

About six months after that conversation with my son, my daughter, who was maybe about 6 or 7 years old at the time, also experienced me not at my finest point. It was bedtime, and we were all trying to calm the house down after a long day. I have a set bedtime routine during which they go to bed at 8:30p.m., they read for 30 minutes, and then, we turn the lights out. After a round of bedtime negotiations and about the third, "It's bedtime," my daughter was still trying to pick a book out to read. This particular day was very tiring and stressful for me. I was commuting to work in a different city, which took about 20 minutes on a good day with no traffic. However, on a regular day with traffic, it took about 2-3 hours. This particular day, I had one of my longer commutes that bordered on 3 hours just to get home. I had a long day at work. I came home, and we had dinner. I cleaned up the house and got the two younger kids showered and situated for bed. The house was finally quieting down for the night. I went into the sunroom to take a moment to reset and just breathe. Our sunroom was a room off the main rooms of the house. It served as our library, computer station, workspace, and game room for the kids. I was sitting there taking a breath, and my daughter walked in the room. She was looking for a book, and she could sense that I was in a mood. At this point, the reality of me being in a mood was becoming more and more normal. She called out to me to ask me a question. I responded to her harshly with, "WHAT!" She put her head down. Still not recognizing what I had done, I said, "WHAT IS IT!" My response was not a question; it was a statement. If I'm honest, at that moment, I really didn't care how I sounded. My need for a quiet moment outweighed her needs. It wasn't that my wanting a moment to myself was bad. The problem was that I crushed her spirit in the process of getting what I wanted. "Be angry but do not sin." (Ephesians 4:26, NLT).

When I finally recognized my tone, I was able to see that her whole demeanor had changed. I asked her to come to me, and I sat her on my lap. I remember having had a conversation with my husband earlier that week. My daughter had shared with him that her older brothers had told her she was annoying. I thought about the statement she shared and my reaction to her. I asked, "Do you think you're annoying?" She just dropped her head, and she just shook it yes. Her eyes began to well up with tears. I asked her, "Do you think that *I think* you're annoying?" She just broke down in tears. She started to just sob, and she shook her head, "Yes." My eyes started to well up with tears. Holding it together, I asked her, "Do you think I like you?," and she shook her head "No." I asked her, "Do you think I love you?," and she shook her head "No" again. My heart dropped to the pit of my stomach. Nothing else mattered in that moment except the fact that I had made my own child feel as though her mother did not like her AND I made her believe that she was annoying to me. Now, I know some of this is open to a child's interpretation, but almost all of her feelings were on me. All I had the capacity to do at that moment was to tell her just how much I loved and liked her, and I tried to reaffirm her.

As a parent, you have to step back and have a truth moment with yourself. I thought, *My God, what is going on right now that I'm just sending the message to my kids that they are a nuisance, that they annoy me, that I don't love them, and that I don't care about them?*

I had to ask myself, *Where are you right now?* I felt just like Adam and Eve in Genesis after they ate the fruit. God came down to the Garden of Eden, and they both hid. God asked, "Where are you?" He was not looking for their physical location. He knew where they were. He wanted to know where they lost their way. Did they understand the fullness of their decision to eat the fruit? Had they realized how far away they became from God in that moment?

I felt so lost. I was never this type of mom. I wasn't this type of woman. What happened? Where was I? I felt exposed. I wanted to cover myself and hide. The disconnect that I felt with having this great life and being a "good mom" was confirmed with the fact that my kids did not feel that this was not the case. I thought, *I'm not crazy. There was a shift. What was happening? Where was this coming from and why? This is who I am, or so I thought.*

When you don't deal with your wounds, you are liable to pass them down from generation to generation. Sometime later, I was picking up my son from work. It was drizzling outside, and it was late. It was close to 1:00a.m. A truck was pulling into an empty parking lot next to me and hit the back side of my car. It was not a hard hit, but it was hard enough to shake the car. A family member was in the back seat at the time of the car accident. I had just purchased the car about 2-3 weeks earlier. We both got out of the car to survey the damage, exchange information, and take pictures. The car had a small scrape, and the bumper was out of alignment. The damage was nothing that required an auto body repair. The person with me had become so upset, that she started slamming her hands on the car, getting in the other driver's face, pointing her finger, and yelling at him at a close range. She had become so upset, so angry, and so enraged very quickly. All I could do was look on and watch her response in awe. Have you ever been in a heated situation and then, there is a calm that comes over you as you watch someone else become enraged? "Fools vent their anger, but the wise quietly hold it back. (Proverbs 29:11, NLT)

Shortly after this minor car accident, I saw my daughter be filled with such hostility, and then, my two of my three boys showed an alarming level of hostility. I determined that this level of anger wasn't going to become a thing that defined my family or my kids! This was not going to happen on my watch! I knew the energy that was around my kids had to change, and that included my energy. It started with my energy. I just didn't know what to do. It's frustrating when you can see the problem and still feel like you still can't do anything about it. You don't have any action steps. You don't have any people you can lean on. When you're new in Christ, you don't really know the Bible. You don't really know how to pray, and all you can think is that there's some special thing that you have to do, and you can't do it. I thought, *God, this is becoming a lot. You're showing me my character, you're confirming it, and now, I'm seeing it play out. God, I just don't know what to do. This is so overwhelming. I'm drowning in myself, and I don't know how to pull myself up for air. It's hard to catch my breath.* That's when things took a turn for the worse, or so I thought.

When I stepped back and observed her shouting at this man, I thought, *This is exactly what my son experienced in the airport. This is what I looked like to my son. I got it! I don't want to be like that. I don't want to become that. I do not want to pass this down to any of my kids. I have to do something about it.* That's when God said to me, "This is how a generational curse looks." I asked God, "If I could fix that in me, is it likely that my kids won't show up like that later?" He said, "Yes." That was what caused my mind to rest. That is where I started to find my resolve.

When people ask me what my "why" is for doing what I do, I tell them I watched a generational curse happen before my eyes. Knowing I could eliminate generational curses instead of passing them to my kids was enough for me. It was important for me to break generational curses. I could leave them with the legacy of good character. That became my "why." In becoming mentally, emotionally, and spiritually healthy and healed, I would set up my future generations for greater success.

Let's Dig:

1.   Have you ever had an experience that you thought
      was justified, only to have someone share that same
      experience from his or her perspective and ask you
      to change or you realized you needed to change?
      What was the situation?
      What needed to change?
      How did it make that person feel?
      How did it make you feel?
      What did you want to change?

2.   Have you ever experienced the realization that you
      make people feel a certain way and you KNEW you
      were in the wrong? Did you rectify it? If not, why?
      If so, what was the outcome? What way did you
      change?

CHAPTER 3

Wounded

SOMETIMES, WE THINK IF we remove ourselves, our problems will go away, but they don't. Undealt with problems always remain a problem.

I've seen many people post how they are moving to new cities, changing their look, and quitting jobs after a bad breakup or challenges at their job and all for the sake of getting rid of problems. What happens when you realize the problem is you?! No matter where you live, how cute your new hair is, or how great the new job is, you still are experiencing the same struggles. You are the common denominator! Ouch! I know, harsh, right? This is exactly where I found myself. I figured if I could just remove certain people, places, and things, my life would be a lot better. It made sense to me. However, as I started to see the fullness of the real me, it didn't matter what I changed around me. I still needed to deal with myself.

Now, I was in a place where my poor performance as a mom, as a wife, and as a woman was confirmed. Things were not going well, and things felt like they were getting progressively worse. All my relationships were suffering. I was longer in communication with my friends like normal, which was unlike our usual constant communication. We went from having girls' nights out or dinner dates to barely even speaking or seeing each other. I stopped being invited to events and felt left out and very alone. I wanted to blame them, but deep down, I knew it was me. I changed.

When someone can see you, like truly see you, they actually can appreciate you for who you are apart from what you can do for them. They can see your inherent value. What happens when you feel unseen? Even though people can see you physically, they no longer see your value. They no longer see how valuable you are, and they lose respect for you. They change the way they handle you and communicate with you. Their desire to connect with you decreases. They even may go as far as speaking to all the things that you are not even though internally, you know there is good in you.

Some people say that people understand from their level of perception. This means they only understand others from the levels they currently understand. If you are healthy, your perception is likely to be healthy, but if you are still operating from your wounds, your perspective is also wounded.

Emotional wounds are wounds that were developed in childhood and possibly nurtured as adults. When you're struggling with one psychological wound, you likely are stepping on other wounds as well, and without identifying them and seeing how they show up in your life, you are likely to operate from a very limited space. How do you even find out what wounds you have? I am glad you asked!

At the start of my journey, one of the first assessments God had me take was to the website of Dr. Jay Earley, the creator of Self-Therapy Journey. Dr. Earley categorizes emotional wounds into four parts:

Harm Wounds

Attack Wound - I was yelled at, hit, or exposed to violence, and now I am afraid of people's anger.

Judgment Wound - I was judged harshly and frequently, and now I feel inadequate and bad about myself.

Shame Wound - I was publicly ridiculed and embarrassed, and now I feel ashamed of myself.

Violation Wound - I was intruded on, smothered, or abused.

Manipulation Wounds

Domination Wound - I was dominated and controlled, and now I allow people to control me or I am afraid of that happening again.

Exploitation Wound - I was used to meet my parent's needs.

Betrayal Wound - I trusted a caregiver and then was betrayed by him or her. Now, I have a hard time trusting anyone.

Guilt Wound - I was repeatedly made to feel guilty about things I did, and now I can't forgive myself.

Rejection Wounds

Rejection Wound - When I reached out for connection, I was dismissed, and now I don't expect people to like me or want me.

Need Wound - I wasn't nurtured and cared for adequately, and now I feel empty and needy.

Abandonment Wound - After being taken care of for a while, I was abandoned, and now I am afraid of being left again.

Not-Seen Wound - I was not seen and appreciated for who I am.

Deficiency Wounds

Basic Deficiency Wound - Because of what happened to me, I feel that I am fundamentally flawed.

Unlovable Wound - Because of what happened to me, I believe that I am not lovable.

Do any of these resonate with you? Did any emotions rise up in you as you read those descriptions? It was the same for me. If you really want to know if categories apply to you, take the Emotional Wounds quiz. This way you'll know for sure the top 3-5 wounds that are connected to you. My wounds were Unseen, Rejection and Abandonment. Naming them is one of the best pieces of information to have when you want to heal and become whole. It equips you with language, and even though they are wounds, you start to believe you can do something about them.

When you haven't taken the time to at least identify what you are dealing with, you can lose hope. Every morning, I started to feel like I got one more day, so I did my best to make it count, but at the end of the day, I still felt defeated.

One day that's where I found myself. I woke up that day and decided I didn't want this anymore. I didn't want to live one more day of this. I did not want to experience one more day of feeling inadequate. One more day of feeling misunderstood. One more day of feeling angry, bitter, and resentful. I had committed that this day would be my last day. Things had gotten so mentally and emotionally bad internally, I just couldn't bear the thought of going on one more day. I figured my family would rally around my kids and take care of them. I had life insurance that would last them for a little while, and I just figured that since I was the problem, if I just removed myself, they wouldn't have to deal with the problem anymore. I would be gone.

I mapped out what I was going to do. It was a Saturday morning. I dropped my kids off at my mom's house and went home. The house was empty. My husband was out running errands for a few hours, and this presented the perfect opportunity. Procrastinating, I cleaned up for a little bit. I then walked throughout the house running my fingers along the walls. I stopped in each room and replayed memories of my family in my mind. I thought about all the good things we did together, all the times that I was a good mother and wife, and all the times that we laughed, and I was able to put a smile on their face. I wanted to have those memories as my last memories and not the ones that made me feel defeated. It's amazing the things we think we can carry with us in those moments.

I made my way to the kitchen, and I grabbed a knife. It was a dull day. There was no sun and no glimmer of hope in the sky. I leaned on the counter and picked up my phone while I still held the knife and scrolled on my phone for a couple minutes. I placed my phone on the counter. I was starting to get nervous a little bit, and my hands started to sweat. I felt my hands getting clammy, and my stomach was getting queasy.

I stood at the counter near the stove, and I raised the knife up to my neck. I thought, *This is going to be quick and easy.*

Do it and be done with it. I pressed the blade right to my neck. It had a sharp edge. It was one of my expensive culinary knives. As I began to give myself a pep talk to go through with my plan, I started to press the knife to my neck harder. Tears started to well up in my eyes, and my throat got tight. I felt like I couldn't breathe. I was not quite crying, but I was emotional because I thought I felt the relief on the other side of what I was attempting to do. I closed my eyes, and tears fell as I pressed the knife against my neck even harder as I got ready to pull the blade across my throat. Then I heard a little whisper in my ear. A voice whispered, "Ask for help." I immediately opened my eyes, and I knew it was God. He sent the Holy Spirit to rescue me. While I still had the knife at my throat and was leaning over on the counter as though I was on auto-pilot, I went to my phone, opened up Facebook, navigated to a Facebook group of wives who were a part of a church where I was a member. I typed the words, "I'm ready to end it. I don't know what to do." I hit enter, and that was it. That was the post. Within minutes, women were texting me, calling me, and responding to my post. They were telling me how loved I was. They were pleading with me not to take my life. They begged me to take a moment to breathe. They asked who they could call or what they could do. One of the women from the group was a therapist, so when she called, I answered. We talked for a few minutes, and her words gave me just enough hope to put the knife down or at the very least remove it from my throat. I took a breath, released the knife, dropped to my knees, and wept.

At that moment, it felt like God scooped me up in the palm of His hand, lifted my face up by my chin, and said, "It's not about the roles you are in. It's neither about the titles you have nor is it about being a mom or a wife." He said, "I designed you to be a woman, and I need you to just be that. I designed you to walk in the Divine power that I've designed women to have. Let's just start there." Then, it was like He put me kind of back down, and for the 30-45 minutes or so, I just wept in the full fetal position on the kitchen floor. God was with me, and God still loved me.

My husband returned home later that evening, but by that time, I had mustered enough strength to shower and get in the bed. I said nothing. I was too ashamed.

They say no weapons formed against you shall prosper. I had never realized that the very weapons that were formed were my own. They were my own thoughts born from my wounds; then, those thoughts became my words, and my words became my actions. Just that quickly, I spiraled out of control. Your wounds will cause you to believe things about yourself, and that becomes the story you tell yourself that becomes *your* truth. Once that false truth gets into your spirit, it can just spiral to a place where you might take any action just to relieve the pain.

Eric Thomas did a talk about bedrock. He equated bedrock to your personal foundation. He talked about how you build on each layer. He said that each layer represents your values, your principles, and your beliefs. It looked a little something like this:

(Insert bedrock photo)

He was making the point that your foundation should be strong enough to sustain you. It brought me back to being on the floor in a fetal position. Sometimes, you just need to hit rock bottom, so that you can be at a level to see the damage and repair the foundation.

I was undoubtedly broken, and I didn't even have a strong enough foundation. That's why it was so easy for me to crumble. The foundation of who you are will crumble if it's not built on solid bedrock or on good soil as the Bible says.

When you're building a house, the first thing that they look at is the soil. As a believer, you are the house in which Christ lives. Although I could see that I didn't have good soil at the time, I was starting to see that I could do something about it.

There are things that you can do to nurture the soil, so it can become the proper bedrock on which to lay the foundation. I cried out to God asking Him to please make me good soil. I wanted him to help me change how I saw myself and help me see my value in the way that He saw me.

He showed me my lack of values, the root of my identity, and the wounds I needed to address. He also showed me how all those things were related and why I was feeling the way I felt.

How does a person lay it down so he or she can have good soil where Christ could come in and build upon it? I knew that if I had the ability to control my thoughts, that meant I had the ability to control my words and my actions. God is so good. He didn't just leave me there.

Prayer

Father God, I pray that any woman who has read up to this point and has resonated with my story will be covered and reminded how loved and valued they are just like you showed me your love. Help them understand that they have a Divine purpose on this Earth because you called them. Give them the strength to keep reading, so they can see that not only can they change their circumstances, but also they can receive exceedingly and abundantly as you have laid the plan for them. Your Word says that if we confess our sins to you, you will be faithful and forgive us our sins and cleanse us from all wickedness (1 John 1:9, NLT). Help us to become good soil, so we can be rooted and planted and bear fruit. In Jesus' name, I pray this prayer. Amen.

Let's Dig:

Head on over to www.selftherapyjourney.com and take the Emotional Wounds Quiz. Come back and write down the top 3-5 wounds here that apply to you:

1.

2.

3.

4.

5.

These will serve as your core wounds. The thought process is that some of your core values are birthed from your core wounds.

Do you have core values? If so, what are they? (Need examples: See Appendix A).

1.

2.

3.

4.

5.

What is it that you believe about yourself (good or bad)?

1.

2.

3.

4.

5.

CHAPTER 4

Light in the Dark

"ONLY IN THE DARKNESS can you see the stars." The late great doctor Martin Luther King said that.

I literally had hit the darkest moment of my life. I attempted to take my life. Things had gotten so bad mentally and emotionally that I just couldn't bear it anymore. The light in my darkest moment was when the Holy Spirit whispered to me to ask for help. That was a light in the dark, a glimpse of hope. Every comment, text, and word of encouragement that came from the women became a star in the dark. God was the one guiding me out of the darkness and into that light. The greatest thing He showed me, as a result of being in that space, was when He said, "It's not about your roles you have. It's not about your titles as a mom or as a wife. It is about who I've designed you to be as a woman, and it wasn't just about you as a woman. It was about all women.

I'm a lover of assessment tools, quizzes, and things where you can collect data about yourself. This is why I encouraged you to go to the site, Self-Therapy Journey, created by Dr. Jay Earley. Self-Therapy Journey is defined as, " an online tool for transforming your psychological issues and enhancing your self-confidence and well-being." This site uses a set of seven different quizzes, and each one provides data or information on your wounds, patterns (behaviors), and capacities.

The emotional wounds are wounds that may have been created in childhood.

The patterns are all the behaviors that came as a result of the wounds, and the capacities are healthy areas of increase that you can activate in your life to help combat the problematic behavior. This is what makes it self-therapy. Each pattern that you display gives you a corresponding capacity in which you need to increase.

It's important that I put this disclaimer in here. This was not a replacement for traditional therapy, and I would strongly recommend that this information be presented to your therapist if you are currently working with one. There is a back end site for licensed therapists where they can access your information. If you are not seeing a mental health professional currently, I would suggest after taking the assessment, especially the wounds assessment, find one that can help you work through it. For the purposes of this book, I will reference mostly patterns and capacities.

Taking the assessment requires the honor system. Your results are based on how truthful your answers are to the questions about where you are in your healing journey and and whether you are willing to be vulnerable. Admit the truth to yourself and answer the questions honestly. If you took the emotional wounds quiz at the end of chapter 3, you can see just how accurate the quiz is. If you haven't taken the quiz yet, go back and take the first of the seven quizzes.

All the quizzes will tell you three things about your results: if you **are** dealing with it, if you **may be** dealing with it, or if you are **not** dealing with it. The quizzes will give you a percentage and a detailed explanation of your results. If there is a pattern that becomes apparent in your data, you will get a corresponding capacity to help with that specific pattern/problematic behavior.

With the emotional wounds quiz, I was able to put a name to the emotional wounds that I had, and that was probably one of the most freeing first steps that I could take. It is important to identify what it is you're experiencing. I didn't know it then, but I was experiencing God's grace and His mercy in my life. "God saved you by his grace when you believed. And you can't take credit for this; it is a gift from God." (Ephesians 2:8, NLT)

What type of emotional wounds could you be dealing with now? If you did the reflection in chapter 3, you have an idea of what those are. The reason why it's called the Self -Therapy Journey is because it guides you enough to be able to identify certain issues you may be experiencing and provides you with valuable resources, tools, and tips.

As I was reading the descriptions from my results of what rejection and abandonment really were and how they showed up in my life, all these stories started to come up from my childhood, and I started to see how all those moments were significant and led up to where I was today. This is why I suggest you couple this survey with therapy or a life coach because there are going to be things that come up that you're going to need to talk about and process though.

I navigated over to the patterns. The patterns are your behaviors. This survey has two focuses.

1. **Interpersonal** - How you relate to **others**
2. **Personal** - How you relate to **yourself**.

It will help you to see how you talk with yourself, how you handle yourself, and what your behavior is like when you're dealing with other people. Let me show you what this looked like for me.

If I'm dealing with a rejection wound and my kids provide me not-so-good feedback as a mom, I would internalize that information, and externally I may become angry (interpersonal pattern) and respond harshly to my kids, while internally, my inner critic (personal pattern) would start to eat at my belief that I could be a good mom. This would then trigger my perfectionism and taskmaster pattern - both personal patterns, and I would try to work to become a "good mom" and do it by ordering tasks that I thought were helping my kids. You probably can see where this is headed. It started to really unravel a lot of the things but provided a lot of answers to the ways that I had been appearing to other people.

Being able to identify the wounds and identify the patterns not only exposes how I'm showing up in the world, but also now I also have an indication of why. What happens next? I mentioned before there was the third quiz, which focuses on capacities. For each pattern it describes a capacity to help you combat that problematic behavior. Praise God! There is an answer key! AMEN!!!

You see, God is not just gonna bring you some place and then leave you. We talked about being in the valley in the beginning of the book. There is hope in the valley, but you're still in the valley. This is why some of the things for which you prayed came with the lessons you weren't prepared to handle. This is where you will discover that there's still some learning that needs to happen. There's still some growth and strengthening that needs to happen. You only get that experience when you're in the valley.

Think about it. When you climb to the top of something, there is nothing left to do but bask in your accomplishment. It was everything you went through to get to the top that made the view from the top all worth it. You want it that way, so when you heal, your character can keep you there. The valley develops good soil, if you let it.

When you get to these high places and you're unable to sustain your foundation, it's going to crumble. That's why being in the valley is important because that's where you will get the knowledge, the skill set, and the strength to be able not only to make it to the mountaintop but also to sustain being there. Moreover, if life happens to dip back into the valley again, you're now equipped with tools that you can use to create a battle kit of spiritual weapons that will help you to continue to move forward. This is a very important part as we move forward. Being equipped with this information, God was really becoming my guide, and I was starting to trust Him.

I remember when I joined the military, the first thing that they teach you is how to be a soldier. Then, they teach you how to do your job for the military. When you go through basic training and learn how to be a soldier, they teach you tactical movements and the ways to use different types of weapons, but they also show you how to guide your way out the wilderness when you are in the field. One of those training exercises occurred when the drill sergeant conducted a mini training on the North Star. He showed us how to find it in the sky and demonstrated how to use it to find your location to guide you.

Yes, you may face obstacles throughout that journey. You may feel lost, but you have a guide, and you have a star that is a light of hope. If you just focus on that, it will lead you to a place where you can start to take steps to your healing journey. That was exactly what God did for me; He became the guide. Right now, He is saying to you, "I will guide you. Just continue to focus on me, listen to my voice, and follow the instructions. Amen" AMEN!

Let's Dig:

Take a moment to pray and reflect, and in your quiet time, ask God these questions and pray these requests and write what comes to your heart. It's ok if you don't hear or feel something immediately. The answers may come over the course of days, weeks or months. It's worth finding out this information. It's freeing, and it's also one jolt of energy to get you going!

1.   Father God, What is your will for my life?
2.   Holy Spirit, can you guide me to and through my path of healing?
3.   Reveal to me the unforgiveness in my heart.
4.   Reveal to me the pride in my heart. (we all deal with it)
5.   Reveal my place in life.
6.   Reveal my purpose in life.
7.   Reveal your provision for my life.
8.   Reveal my identity in You.
9.   What light could He be trying to bring in your life?

CHAPTER 5

The Language of You

"FOR WE KNOW IN part and we prophesy in part, but when completeness comes, what is in part disappears. When I was a child, I talked like a child, I thought like a child, I reasoned like a child. When I became a man, I put the ways of childhood behind me. For now we see only a reflection as in a mirror; then we shall see face to face. Now I know in part; then I shall know fully, even as I am fully known. (1 Corinthians 13:9-12, NIV)

ARTICULATE: The ability to express your thoughts and ideas clearly, easily, and well.

I'm a word nerd. Yep! I am one of those people who loves to look up the definitions of words and find the synonym, the antonym, the root meaning, and sometimes, the Hebrew, Greek and/or Biblical context. There's something in the power of having the right language and the right words to be able to articulate clearly what it is that you want to say whether it is about your feelings or an explanation of something.

From the vantage points of different people, the same word or phrase can mean something completely different. We tend to use the context of that word to give it meaning, and that may not be what someone else thinks it means. I remember a time when I was feeling overwhelmed. I was talking to my husband about how I was feeling, and he asked me what being overwhelmed meant to me. It took a couple of days, but here is what I was able to determine as the meaning for that term and a few other terms. Here were the meanings that I inferred:

Overwhelmed: You have too many problems coming your way and not enough solutions.

Frustrated: There are too many thoughts happening in my own head. I feel stuck and can't seem to process the words I need to express where I am or what I'm feeling.

Annoyed: I'm not getting what I want, or what I think should be happening is not happening

Agitated: When a situation keeps rubbing me the wrong way, and it starts to affect my whole being. I'm losing control over how I feel about the situation. I'm being pulled in so many different directions emotionally, mentally, or physically. This is similar to how the washer machine moves the detergent through the clothes to clean them. It agitates the clothes, so the cleaning solution can get to all the parts of the clothes.

Aggravated: My emotions have clouded my ability to see clearly. I can't see past my own emotions.

Having a definition for a word, outside of what Merriam Webster tells us is huge. Other people now have a clear point of reference for where you are and what you mean. Sometimes, when we need help, we'll just say what we feel, but people do not really know what we're requesting or what we need. Other people have to try to figure it out, and we end up blaming them for not meeting our needs when we really just couldn't describe where we were and what we needed. It's like walking into a store and being asked if you need help, and you say that you do, but you say nothing else after that. Then, you get mad because they aren't helping you with what you need. Once I was able to start gathering meaning to what I was feeling, naming my emotional wounds, describing my behavior, understanding why I was behaving that way, and articulating it, I started to regain control over myself. I felt the power in my voice coming back. That was the power from all those self-therapy assessments.

With this newly found power and feeling of being back in control, I was introduced to the concept of boundaries. I'll be honest. I had none. I didn't even know what they were or why I needed them. Now, I've heard people say things like, "You don't have to take or accept that" and "You don't deserve to be treated like that." I even have heard people say, "You need to put your foot down." However, I never knew these statements were wrapped up in boundaries. I knew the next steps were going to be learning, understanding, and implementing boundaries.

I was in a counseling session, and my therapist and I were talking about boundaries and walking through that process of establishing boundaries. She provided me with a worksheet to process this concept. The worksheet identified three types of boundaries and 6 categories:

Types of Boundaries

- **Flexible**: The person's boundary is neither too closed nor too open.
- **Permeable**: The person's boundary is too open
- **Rigid**: The person's boundary is too closed

Categories boundaries are implemented:

1. **Physical Boundaries**: Physical boundaries include your needs for personal space, your comfort with touch, and your physical needs like needing to rest, eat food, and drink water.

2.   **Emotional Boundaries**: Emotional boundaries are all about respecting and honoring feelings and energy.

3.   **Time Boundaries**: Your time is valuable, and it is important to protect how it is utilized.

4.   **Sexual Boundaries**: Healthy sexual boundaries include consent, agreement, respect, understanding of preferences and desires, and privacy

5.   **Intellectual Boundaries**: Intellectual boundaries refer to your thoughts, ideas, and curiosity.

6.   **Material Boundaries**: Material boundaries refer to items and possessions like your home, car, clothing, jewelry, furniture, money, etc.

I remember a coworker telling me that I could be really good at what I did if I wasn't so rigid. At the time, I didn't even know what that meant, but it stayed with me. My immediate thought was, "I'm not rigid!" When I started learning boundaries, I thought about what she said. I looked up the definition of rigid and it said: *unable to bend or be forced; not able to be changed or adapt.* I'll be honest. There are certain ways about me because I know where I can be stuck in that way of thinking. I can be unwilling to yield to a different way of thinking, and sometimes, I struggle to be flexible. I can be rigid sometimes. When I applied that definition to setting my boundaries, I could see how it made it hard for people to be in a relationship with me because of my unwillingness to be flexible.

If I hadn't taken the time to study what boundaries are and what they do in conjunction with what it meant to me to be rigid I wouldn't have taken the time to see just how difficult I had become. When establishing my boundaries, the goal is to be as flexible as I can be in most areas. That is different from being permeable. Being permeable is the equivalent of being a people-pleasing doormat! We don't want that!

When you know the words and phrases that clearly and easily define what you want to say, no one can take that away from you. You own it! You own that information.

Nobody can go into your brain and say, "Give me that back! Where they do that at?!" Once it is locked in, it is one thing that people cannot take away from you. This is why the more that you know about yourself, the less likely it is for someone to be able to come in and tell you who you are. PERIOD!

When I was taking the assessments on wounds, patterns, and capacities, there was one other assessment I took. It was the DISC assessment. The DISC assessment is an observable behavioral profiling system which measures the energy you are putting into (D) Dominating problems, (I) Influencing people, (S) Steadying the environment, and (C) Complying to rules and details. It helps you to recognize your own behavioral and communicative style, see what works and doesn't work, and identify areas of growth. It tells others how to communicate with you, anticipates tension in relationships, and shows you how to read others and adapt your communication. The DISC assessment measures your underlying emotions, needs, and fears (like an iceberg), and identifies the primary concerns that drive all behavior.

There was a gentleman by the name of Chris Daniel, who has since passed away, who took the basic DISC assessment and broke it down in terms of animals. He associated an animal to each letter of the DISC assessment. He started during the facilitation of DISC assessment to ESL speakers at an airport and became aware of the language barrier that existed. One thing he knew they had in common was that they both had a general understanding of animal characteristics. For the D in DISC, he assigned it a gorilla because of the aggressiveness, assertiveness, directness ,and results-oriented nature and presence of a gorilla. For the I in DISC, he assigned it a flamingo which is more social, influential, and emotional. For the S in DISC, he assigned it a chameleon for being adaptable, stable due to its ability to blend in, and systematically approach. For the C in DISC, he assigned it a turtle because of its need to process based on compliance and rules and regulations; they process things in a very strategic way and appear to move slightly slower than the rest of the other animals. He called his

version of the assessment, The 4Animals Experience . Just
before he passed away, I became a certified trainer in The
4AnimalsExperience and later in the DISC assessment.

When I took the assessment and received my report
back, I looked at it. It gives you two sets of numbers for each
letter in the DISC assessment. You're natural and adaptive.
My results showed I had a low score on D (23/100), and my
I and my S were the same across the assessment (67/100).
I had a slightly higher score on C (77/100). My primary
animal was a Turtle! I actually put the assessment down
because folks who were taking the assessment at the same
time were scoring 99% in certain letters, and I was just
average, or so I thought. I later learned that having I,S, and
C within 10 points of each other was rare and not too many
people display results that way.

A few months later, God had me go back and look
at my results - like really look at them. He had me read
through the characteristics of each behavioral trait and the
communication descriptions. My results confirmed even
more about the patterns (behaviors) from my wounds. All
wounds have triggers, and this helped me see many of
those triggers in behaviors and communication. I read how
I showed up when I was under stress, and it revealed my
communication strengths and challenges. It even shared the
best ways people could communicate with me. There were
things that I believed were flaws because of how people

made fun of them. Some things about me rubbed people the wrong way, or I was labeled, "teacher's pet, overachiever, or doing the most." These attributes were the very things that made me, ME! God said, "I want you to think back to the way that you learn and the way that you are with your kids. I want you to think back to how you operate in your career. You always tend to teach. You select careers where there is an exactness or compliance to them. There's always a process, and there's always a system."

He fashioned me in a way that confirmed this was exactly who I was meant to be. This revelation gave me a whole new level of confidence. I told myself, *This is exactly who you are.* I had new language and terminology to use. It was blowing my mind. Now, I have my wounds. I have my patterns, and I have my capacities. Now I also have an assessment that says this is how you behave and how you communicate. I mean this was like the sweet package that detailed me. I was given the blueprint to myself. No one could convince me of anything different. My flaws were right there! My wounds were right there! My value was right there!

I could walk in that authority. It created this level of self-ownership that I didn't have previously. The opinion of other people no longer could seep into my spirit and transform the way I saw myself. It no longer could devalue me because I had something that showed me my value. It freed me from the trap of other people's stinking thinking. I was beginning to walk in the authority of who I was and how God designed me to be.

Having these 4 assessments helped remove some of the guilt and shame that people placed on me simply because I didn't do something that they wanted me to do. Instead, I walked in what was true to me.

Going through this process is not just for you. It's also for your relationships. I was able to become a better mom, wife, and woman because now I could show up as the true authentic version of myself. When I was rescued from my suicide attempt, God said it was not about my roles or my titles. It was about becoming the woman I was designed to be with the Divine purpose God has given me. Having these assessments in hand allowed me to do that. I was equipped with more tools that strengthened and encouraged me. Because I could own myself and see my intrinsic value, I could let go of the titles and roles and just be me. From that moment forward, I became a mom who used teaching as a method of parenting. I allowed myself space to be able to be social with them and engage with them, but I did it in a way that not only met their needs, but also it met my needs. Now, they have consistency in my behavior. They know exactly when I'm upset and why I am upset, and instead of being that woman who I was in the airport, I can now sit down with them and say, "I'm disappointed and here's why" without damaging them, harming them, or putting them in a compromising situation where they feel like now they have to parent me because I'm emotionally immature. They can still be the kid, and I can still be the parent. Both of us have our integrity and our character intact.

The power of walking authentically as yourself because of who you are and because you can articulate who you are, removes any shame, guilt, or inadequacy that we feel.

I want to encourage you at this moment to find a way that you can assess who you are. There are more resources at the end of this book that I have found extremely helpful. I have facilitated over 100 assessments that help women gain personal freedom and become the women they desire to be. Find what works for you. It's time to move forward and grow, evolve, and become the woman God designed you to be. This could be the defining moment that could shift your life forever.

Let's Dig:

Do you currently have boundaries in place that you can articulate clearly? If so, list three of those boundaries:

1.

2.

3.

In each category, circle where you currently are with your boundaries and select where you would like to be:

Boundary Category	Current	Future
Physical Boundaries	Rigid Flexible Permeable	Rigid Flexible Permeable
Emotional Boundaries	Rigid Flexible Permeable	Rigid Flexible Permeable
Time Boundaries	Rigid Flexible Permeable	Rigid Flexible Permeable
Sexual Boundaries	Rigid Flexible Permeable	Rigid Flexible Permeable
Intellectual Boundaries	Rigid Flexible Permeable	Rigid Flexible Permeable
Material Boundaries	Rigid Flexible Permeable	Rigid Flexible Permeable

CHAPTER 6

The Capacity to Live

THERE IS A MOVIE called, *Now You See Me*. It is about a group of magicians who create optical illusions as part of their acts. They would be standing in one place one minute, and then poof, they would disappear. Then, they would reappear in another place and you would think, *Clearly, they couldn't have been in two places at once.* Teleporting is not possible, at least that we know of. How did they get from one place to the other? They were either there or they weren't there, and that reality creates this illusion. The challenge is figuring out what is real. How did they even do that? What steps did they have in place to even map that out in their heads? What was their process to be able to plan one thing in one place and plan something in another place? How do they even create a strategy? It's likely they had a vision, and they knew they wanted to execute it, so they came up with a strategy.

Lee Bolman said, "A vision without a strategy remains an illusion." Do you have a vision for how you want to show up as a woman, as a mother, or a wife, even if you currently aren't one? Can you articulate it, make it plain, and share the vision with others? Sometimes, we look at ourselves, and we think we're one person when we're really not one person. Therefore, we pretend that we are that person, yet we live it out in such a way that it creates an illusion for other people.

I remember when my friends started to say, "You're a supermom. You can do all the things." I started to live up to the hype that I was a supermom, and I could do all things and be all places at one time. I believed that I could be the wife who had dinner on the table, kept the house clean, supported my husband, and functioned as the helpmeet that God said I was supposed, all while being this polished Proverbs 31 woman. I thought that I could do it all, and I could have it all until I realized it was just an illusion. Everything I was being sold was based on their perception of me, but it was not the truth. I had to accept I wasn't the polished Proverbs 31 woman. I wasn't a supermom, and I wasn't the ultimate helpmeet that I thought I was portraying. I bought into this dream believing that women are supposed to be superwomen. They're supposed to have it all. They're supposed to be able to manage it all, and they're supposed to be able to maintain it all. Then, it got real. The illusion was ripped from my eyes, and I found myself in a place where I was asking what was the truth. How was I supposed to get from under this supermom mantra that was the model to which I aspired and just be myself, especially, when I felt pressured to be a certain type of woman, wife, and mother. All I wanted to do was just be myself.

One night as I was in my quiet time with God, He said, "You don't need to be a supermom, but you should be a super mom, and you can be that through me." I couldn't do all things in my own strength, but I could with His strength. I just sat for a minute with that. It's not supermom (one word). It's a super mom (two words). It just rocked my world. It is the same word separated by a tiny little space. I just had to be a super mom - meaning I just had to give the best of what I had naturally to give, and I knew I could be one with God. You don't have to be a superwife; you just have to be a super wife. You don't have to be the wife who washes every dish, launders every piece of clothing, and keeps the house spotless to be the perfect wife. Be the wife who shows up committed every day flawed but progressing. Be the wife who commits to helping in ways that she speaks to her husband but are also authentic to you. Commit to being the mom who wants to read the book at the end of the night 10 minutes past bedtime because the relationship that's being solidified at that moment is more important. But most importantly, be committed to the woman you desire to become.

I was in a group at work that was run by a Ph.D. candidate intern. The work group was catered to the women of color who worked for the organization. It was a safe space to talk, share, vent and just be. There was no judgment and no shame in the group. The leader always opened up with a poem or some word of encouragement. One particular day, she opened up with Nikki Giovanni's poem entitled "WOMAN."

She wanted to be a blade
of grass amid the fields
but he wouldn't agree
to be a dandelion
She wanted to be a robin singing
through the leaves
but he refused to be
her tree
She spun herself into a web
and looking for a place to rest
turned to him
but he stood straight

declining to be her corner
She tried to be a book
but he wouldn't read
She turned herself into a bulb
but he wouldn't let her grow

She decided to become
a woman
and though he still refused
to be a man
She decided it was all
right

My takeaway from the poem was this. People can and may refuse to be the support you need to grow into the woman you desire to be, but when you realize that the only person who can help you change is you, you'll make the decision to become the woman you desire to be, and it will be alright. She decided that she was going to be a woman. There is a popular quote that I keep in my battle kit, "She believed she could, so she did." Just like the woman in the poem, she believed. Become her at the best level that you can. That defines your level of super.

Who you think you are and who you think you aren't are both right. I thought I was supposed to be this supermom, ultimate helpmeet, Proverbs 31 woman, but I also knew how hard it was to live up to that expectation and standard, and both were right. I was putting my energy and my emphasis on the roles and the titles and was trying to live up to some ideologies that were not authentic to me. However, when I switched it and put away my childish thinking, and I put the emphasis on just being me and really just being the best woman I could be, I could become the mom and wife I desired to be. There was one other assessment I took that I didn't discuss in much detail, but it was one of the most beneficial tools for me. In fact, it was where my professional title, The Capacity Coach, was born. The assessment is called Capacities. Capacities are abilities that you could increase in areas such as patience, ease, clarity, courage, or cooperation. Capacities affect how we are with ourselves and how we are with others, which is similar to our patterns/behaviors. When you increase your capacity, your core problematic behavior patterns will decrease simply because you have developed a healthy capacity that can take you to the next level. Then, it clicked! That's the strategy! That is the strategy I would need to implement to achieve the vision of the woman I desired to be. Based on the vision of the type of woman I desired to be and the type of woman I was designed to be, I was now equipped with capacities that could get me there.

Below are some examples of personal (how you are with yourself) and interpersonal (how you are with others) health capacities.

Personal Capacities:

1. **Clarity Capacity**: I can think clearly and stay focused even in difficult situations.
2. **Courage Capacity**: I have the courage to take the risks to move my life ahead.
3. **Ease Capacity**: I feel confident and at ease in my work.
4. **Responsibility Capacity**: I feel empowered and in charge of my life.
5. **Self-Esteem Capacity**: I feel good about myself.

Interpersonal Capacities

1. **Centered Capacity**: I can stay cool even when my anger is triggered.
2. **Cooperation Capacity**: I am open to other people's opinions and can work well with them.
3. **Self-Care Capacity**: I am in touch with my own needs and desires.
4. **Self-Support Capacity**: I feel whole even when my partner is away or distant.

Let's Dig:

Looking at some of the capacities listed above. What are two capacities that stand out to you in which you would like to increase? If you took the assessments, what are the first two capacities identified in your results?

Personal Capacities:

1.
2.

Interpersonal Capacities:

1.
2.

CHAPTER 7

Ezer - The Warrior Within

STUPID IS KNOWING THE truth, seeing the truth, and still believing the lies. I am not stupid.

One day, during my devotional time, He said, "Yes I created the world in six days and saw that it was good. Yes, I created man in my image and saw that it was good, but when I saw a man alone, it was not good. There was something that I did to make it good." Then, He asked me, "What did I do next?" I said, "Well, when you saw that it wasn't good for man to be alone, you made... and the light bulb went off...you made a woman! You didn't make another man! You didn't make a child! You didn't make another tool or animal; You MADE A WOMAN! I thought, *Oh my God! I'm good! That's the truth! I was needed!*

That's the truth! He designed me to help! That's the truth! Sis, do you see just how valuable you are! You were designed ON purpose and FOR a purpose. God wanted you here! He knew that a WOMAN would be needed. With His power, He empowered you with an undeniable strength, courage, and wisdom.

I'm not *just* a mom. I'm *a* mom, and THAT'S THE TRUTH! I'm not some subservient wife. I'm the helper, and THAT'S THE TRUTH! He knew that the man was going to need help, and what's interesting about this is He didn't need this masculine energy. He didn't need someone who could come alongside him and cut down trees and manage the garden or do all this heavy lifting. No, He knew that He needed a gentle but strong source of strength and help. He needed someone who could come alongside and speak the truth in love and be peace in love. He needed someone who might come alongside man and be the mirror and the reflection. He needed someone who could come alongside man and be the emotional support and strength when man would need it the most. He wanted someone who could be with man and be a source of comfort, vulnerability, and softness.

Society has made it seem like women are weak, or it has set the standards and expectations of a woman so low that I had developed this masculine energy to compete with the man because, in my mind, we were the same, and

I refused to be treated just any kind of way. God quickly checked me when I exposed this belief and said, No, no, no. Don't go down that path; don't start thinking those thoughts. You are the same because you are both flesh, but I have designed you in two totally different ways and for totally different reasons."

I started to do more research on what help and support means. Here is what I found:

Help: *Verb* - to make it easier for someone to do something by offering one's services or resources; to serve. *Noun* - the action of helping someone to do something; assistance.

Support: *Verb* - bear all or part of the weight of; hold up. *Noun* - a thing that bears the weight of something or keeps it upright.

Now think about that? Based on those two definitions, do you know how much strength He had to give us to help others and be a source of support? There is a common theme that exists across all definitions of the word, *strength*. The common theme reflects the ability to show up and be there in the moments when others were not as strong for themselves.

Do you know what kind of strength it takes for you to have to pray on behalf of your children when they're being disrespectful?

Do you know what kind of strength it takes when your child is going in a way in which you did not train him or her and you don't know what to do and all you can do is pray?

Do you know what kind of strength it takes to pray for your marriage when you're not sure which way it's going to go and all you have is hope and faith that things will turn around and get back on track?

Do you know what kind of strength it takes when you want to quit but you have to keep going?

Do you know what kind of strength it takes to commute every day 2 hours in traffic to an unfulfilling job and come home and muster enough energy to hug your children, kiss your husband, and attempt to get a hot dinner on the table?

Do you know what kind of strength it takes day in and day out to do laundry, clean the house, go food shopping, and make sure everybody is up-to-date with school, medical, and dental appointments?

Do you know what kind of strength it takes to work a 9-5 job when you're not being paid what you're worth and you know you deserve more? Do you know how it feels when you decide to start a business and when you come home after working all day, make a long commute home, tend to the house, and put the kids to bed, and you still stay up until 1:00a.m. to work on your business?

Do you know what kind of strength it takes to be the COO of your household and in some cases the CEO of your household? Do you know how it feels to try continuously to stay abreast of what's happening in your household?

Do you know what kind of strength it takes to continue to seek God and nurture that spiritual relationship despite your own uncertainty?

Do you know what kind of strength it takes to just show up everyday despite everything that you are experiencing?

This list is exhaustive, but you are still here aren't you? Do you know what kind of strength it takes? I do. It takes a Warrior kind of strength.

I never fully understood the term "helpmeet" or "helpmate." You know me. I did more research! Aren't you glad to have someone like me come along and do all this research? Now, we both can learn! As I was studying, I came across the term "Ezer Kenegdo" quite a few times.

Ezer Kenegdo. Ezer Kenegdo is the Hebrew word for "helpmeet." God designed women to be a helpmeet. In Hebrew, it means: to rescue/to save and to be strong. This term, "Ezer," was only used a handful times in military context in the Bible. However, there was this one time it wasn't used in that context and guess when that was? That time was when God made Eve and referred to her as an "Ezer" or "helpmeet." The Ezer is a Warrior. You are a Warrior. You are an Ezer, a strong Warrior who is complementary to man.

We are a strong helper and Warrior for Christ. However, we have to make sure we don't get ahead of ourselves and think we are better than another person. Mikella Van Dyke said it best with this explanation:

"The word that accompanies ezer is kenegdo which means "in front of him,"'opposite as to him' or 'corresponding as to him'. A great visual explanation of the word kenegdo would be two wings on a bird, they are not the same, but are equal. They correspond to each other, both are useful for flight, but they are not identical. When both are used together they accomplish one purpose, movement towards Christ. Kenegdo denotes the idea of equality, a mirror image of a man, but the opposite of him.

As women, we are often declared the "weaker sex," but this is not how God sees us. He sees us as Warrior's in battle. Women who are strong fortresses with our men, a savior in times of trouble. Jesus had many women that he called to battle. One of these was his own mother, Mary. Mary gave up everything to follow God. She was strong, and able. Ruth and the Proverbs 31 woman are called women of valor. This term is ALSO a military term uses to describe strength, might, armies, and force." - Mikella Van Dyke

The strength that He's given to women is equivalent to the strength of a Warrior. My God! Women are Warriors! Honey, I stepped right into my royalty as the daughter of a King.

I'm a Warrior. You are a Warrior! We are Warriors in Womanhood!

Resting on that truth, I fully and wholeheartedly understood what it means when they say, "The truth will set you free." There were chains breaking off of my belief and my identity. There were things that I had held onto for so long. Remember, I said that what you think you are and what you think you aren't are both, right? Everything that I thought I wasn't was breaking off of me, so everything I knew could attach to me.

Warriors cannot walk in bondage. Warriors cannot walk with their hands shackled; they cannot walk with their feet shackled. How do you fight the good fight when your mind and your heart are in bondage with soul ties wrapped around them? How?

It was never about being in the role of a mom. It was never about having the title of a wife, employee, director, or leader. It was more about discovering His divine power and purpose for women and of womanhood.

That was the only thing specific to me. The way in which I would walk out his Divine purpose in me only was going to come out in a way that spoke to me, and that's the exact same for you! That's why it doesn't make sense to hate on other women because whatever they have wasn't for you. Otherwise, what they have would have been given to you.

I thought back about what a Proverbs 31 woman is, and there were 10 characteristics that defined her:

1. She is faithful to Jesus and loves Him.
2. She is a faithful wife
3. She is a loving mother, and her children call her blessed.
4. She takes care of her physical, mental, and spiritual health.
5. She serves others with love and kindness.
6. She is a wise steward of the gifts God has given her.
7. She is industrious and works with willing hands.
8. She is a good manager of her home.
9. She spends her time on that which is good.
10. She is creative and embraces beauty and godliness.

I looked at all these characteristics. We, as women, have the ability to step into every one of these roles and do well in it. God told me it wasn't just for me. It was to let any woman with whom I am in contact know she does have the power and the ability too because they were Divinely assigned to her. There's nothing she can do to get rid of it; it was Divinely assigned. Now, she can ignore it, but she can't get rid of it.

When you walk in your Divine assignment, and she walks in her Divine assignment, and you two come together, my God! We're talking about building an army of Women Warriors for the Kingdom. When we get it together, we can lock arm and arm. We can go out on the spiritual battlefield and battle things together and triumph. We are more than conquerors. Isn't that what the Book says? How can we conquer anything when we are not willing to accept the truth, create the vision and the strategy, and walk in the process.

Prayer:

Father God, I just thank you for the woman reading this right now. May you expose in her what you exposed in me. Help her to see her identity in you. An identity rooted in courage, strength, wisdom and purpose. May she learn to walk in YOUR truth of who she truly is and let go of what the world has told her she is or needs to become. Help her release the strongholds that are keeping her weighed down. Remove the beliefs that have challenged her when she knows in her heart of heart she is more precious than a jewel. Remind her of her unique design and allow her to walk in that design with grace, humility, and mercy. I pray for her. We are her. In Jesus's Name. Amen.

Let's Dig:

It's about your character and your heart.

What do you believe? Are you willing to believe that God designed you with a strength that no one can come against?

Are you willing to believe that you have a Divine purpose on this Earth?

Are you willing to believe that the strength that He gave you was the same strength that was designed for Warriors?

Are you willing to believe that you are a Warrior? Well, are you?

*No one can take your value.
You were born with it!*

CHAPTER 8

Kintsugi - Beautifully Broken

I READ A BOOK CALLED, *The End of Me*, by Kyle Idleman. The title alone got me. At the beginning of the book, he talks about the moment when Jesus becomes real. He says there's a moment that you hit when you come to the end of yourself, and Jesus takes over. For me, that was my suicide attempt. That was the end of me, and that's when Jesus took over. Another concept he taught in his book was this Japanese art style called Kintsugi. Kintusgi is the ancient art of repairing broken pottery with gold or silver. The cracks are viewed as part of the history of the object, and they are not treated as though they are something to hide. The pottery ends up being more valuable when it is repaired with the gold than it is in its original state.

Think about it this way. You take a bowl and drop it, and it cracks to about 10-20 pieces. It is broken enough that it needs to be repaired. You really want to make sure that it's secure, so after you glue the pieces back, you carefully go over each sealed crack with liquid gold. What was once a plain white cereal bowl is now solidified with liquid gold. How much more valuable do you think that Dollar Tree cereal bowl became when you added the liquid gold to it to seal the broken pieces?

It is the same thing God does with us. God sees how broken we are. He sees all the cracks and damage we have, and instead of throwing us away, He steps in with his liquid gold, and He purposefully and carefully seals us back together. We become more valuable because we have the experiences of our brokenness that had been sealed and healed by the grace and mercy of God. Kintsugi is the thing that gave me a picture of what my heart looks like as it's being repaired. God is picking up the pieces and putting it back together; He is sealing it with His truth. He seals my identity in Him. He seals my ability to pray. He shows me He is with me every step of the way, and every time He does that, He continues to add liquid gold to seal the broken pieces of my heart, my being, my spirit, my body, my mind, and my soul. It's not something that special to me. It's what He does for anybody who seeks His face.

It's what He did in the story of the Potter's House. The Potter was working with the clay. The clay just buckled, so he did it again this time, but he did it better than he did the first time. When we are in God's hands, the One who's fashioned us, He has done it before. We were born into a broken world. He's gonna need to do it again, except this time, He is going to do it with liquid gold. He is going to make the gold stick because once we know who He is, He knows we don't need to be convinced, swayed, manipulated, misguided, sneaked, snaked, or bamboozled. We know exactly who He is.

I remember listening to an episode on Focus on the Family, and Patsy Clairmont was talking about her book, *God Uses Cracked Pots*. On this particular episode, they aired one of her previous talks related to her book. She talked about how we think we might be damaged goods and feel we're not usable or that we cannot be a part of God's Kingdom. This was something I believed. *God doesn't want a damaged woman like me*, I would say to myself. *He doesn't want somebody who's wishy-washy in her faith. He doesn't want somebody who is just a fan. He wants a follower*. However, she talked about how even though the pot might be damaged, it still works. It still can be used.

No matter how damaged, broken, or flawed we think we are, we are beautifully broken because you are beautifully healed. You are sealed. You are more valuable than you ever could imagine. I knew this because He started to solidify my identity in Him and not in the world, not in what people thought of me, not in what my kids thought of me, and not even in what my husband thought of me. I no longer cared about what my kids thought about me because their opinions didn't determine my value because I was rooted in the truth. I started with a scripture a day based on a topic or theme followed by prayer. The very first 30-day scripture that He started me with was, *My Identity in Christ.* Each day, I read a scripture that related to who I was in Him.

This is where my Warrior journey started. I could become her. She wasn't some far-off Proverbs 31 woman. I could become her. I was becoming her.

I briefly mentioned this in a previous chapter. I had my battle kit. I started building a battle kit of spiritual tools. In order for me to walk this out, I was going to need spiritual weapons, so if I stumbled or started to feel those angry emotions well back up, I could just pick a tool and center myself.

Affirmations were my biggest tool and weapon! You know I never understood the power of an affirmation, the power of words, the power of language, or the power of speaking things out loud until I knew that it could check my emotions, remove my flesh, and put me back in the presence of God. We talk about affirmations, and we talk about having scripture and all these things in place, but really, we don't show what it looks like when we say it. We feel good in the five seconds that it comes from our mouths, but really, what we're doing in those moments is reminding ourselves that Jesus died on the cross for us, so who am I to go out and speak horribly of somebody else, and He died for me? We think, *Oh, so now because my feelings are hurt, I feel like I can go out and be reckless with my mouth.* Sis, that's not why He died for us. That math doesn't add up. Not even that new math can help that interpretation. That's the power of affirmations when you're willing to have the affirmations backed up by the Holy Spirit that can take the enemy down and not take root in you.

What was I going to put in this battle kit? Your battle kit is built with three categories in mind. Most of you have many of these items, but you are just not using them intentionally. They are people, places and platforms, and things.

People: There are select people you should be able to lean on when you are fighting against your flesh. Here are mine: a therapist, an elder woman/spiritual mom, a community of like-minded women, and accountability partners. Notice, I didn't say family or friends. It doesn't mean that some of these people may not fall into that category. It means that I am intentional about whom I go to with my struggles, and it's not always family and friends.

Places and Platforms: I often take a walk or clean when I am dealing with something, and my emotions are running high. There are a couple of parks and an ice cream spot that I frequent. I also love to swim, so the local YMCA is also a location I visit to decompress. Sometimes, I take a long hot shower or soak in the tub. These all seem like basic places, but they are identified as battle kit locations. They become intentional in my journey. Platforms such as Netflix, Pureflix, and even Youtube can help me take my mind to other places. Your platforms (digital locations) may be different. Maybe it's Etsy or Amazon. It's a place where you can go that will help you take your mind off what's happening, settle your emotions, and ground yourself, so you can come back and fight the battle more effectively.

Things (Tips, Tools, and Techniques): For me, this is music and more music. I love to sing and dance. Worship, Soca and the Beyonce station on Pandora and Amazon are my go to music sources when I'm in a mood. I love wall art with cute sayings and reminders of who is in control. I would just print them out at Wal-Mart and pin them up. I put scripture in my battle kit. I started to pray more. I started talking to God in the way in which I spoke, I didn't make it super sweet or deep. I just came to Him as myself right where I was.

These were all things that I used to help me fight against mental, emotional, physical, financial, relational, and spiritual battles.

Remember when we talked about that good soil? Well, here it is. This is what it looks like once you clean up the wounds, change your behaviors, and intentionally prepare the soil, so seeds can be planted. I can start to bear fruit from what I'm learning and now, I can plant seeds in other women.

My words are changing. My thoughts are changing. My actions are changing. None of us are immune to life's brokenness. When we are restored, that is where the beauty lies. Brokenness leaves its mark, but if we choose, our lives can be changed for the better.

Let's Dig:

In the beginning of the chapter, we talked about coming to the end of ourselves. What is that moment for you?

When you look at what you're bearing right now, is it the fruit you can share? If not, what would you like to change?

Remember: You are beautifully broken. Your wounds will turn into wisdom.

CHAPTER 9

Arm Her - The Battle Kit

A STUDENT SAYS TO HIS master, 'You talk about peace but teach me fighting. How do you reconcile the two?" The master replied, "It's better to be a Warrior in a garden than a gardener in a war."

God was teaching me to own myself, walk in my purpose, and understand who I am, so I could be at peace with myself.At the same time, He was preparing me for spiritual warfare should and when it would come. He was teaching me a Warrior's mindset and He wanted me to be prepared for the battlefield of the mind. Offenses will come, and that's why I need you to be prepared. You need to have a level of peace about who you are and whose you are.

When the offenses come, you know which ones to go to battle for and which ones to ignore. That you have the ability to equip yourself. It wasn't just about having my battle kit of prayer, word studies, scriptures, sermons, and music and community. It wasn't just those things. I've allowed these offenses to come and attack my thoughts, I also gave them permission to be there, and now, it's time to defeat the enemy. We are more than conquerors, but first, you need to know that you can conquer the enemy. What exactly is it that you are trying to conquer? Remember, a vision without a strategy is just an illusion. Without a clear vision, you may end up fighting the wrong fight and with the wrong tools. You only can conquer that for which you are prepared. Someone who's not only equipped but also has the right tools is likely to become a conqueror because he or she is prepared and is rooted in and with God. People still can pray and have all the tools, but if they are rooted in the world, they only can conquer wordly battles. That's exhausting. For them, it's always going to be situation to situation and circumstance to circumstance. However, when you are rooted in Christ, you eliminate that situation, so you don't have to deal with it anymore. Remember your armor from Ephesians 6:10-18 (NIV).

Natalie Regoli, Editor in Chief at Connect Us Fund, gives a great definitions of each:

#1: The Belt of Truth: Truth is the belt that holds armor together. We must know God's truth in order to protect ourselves against our flesh, the world, and the enemy. Truth grounds us and reminds us of our identity in Christ.

#2: The Breastplate of Righteousness: As Jesus's followers, we have no righteousness apart from what has been given to us by God. Our breastplate is His righteousness, and His righteousness will never fail. It is by His power we chose to do right. Living a right life and being rooted in God's Word is powerful in protecting our heart, killing our flesh, and defeating the enemy.

#3: Shoes of Peace: They have a firm foundation. We need a firm foundation in Jesus. We have peace in knowing we are secure in what Jesus has done for us.

#4: Shield of Faith: Faith is the shield for us. Trusting in God's power and protection is so important. When the battle gets worse, we must remember that God works all things for good. He is always true to His promises.

#5: Helmet of Salvation: This is the most crucial piece of armor for us. Without the Holy Spirit, all other armor is useless. Salvation empowers believers to fight. It protects us in our weaknesses. Without salvation, there is no victory. Without the Holy Spirit guiding us, there is no vision, and there is no strategy.

#6: Sword of the Spirit: Our sword is the Word of God. Every other piece of armor protects us against attacks, but with God's Word, we are able to fight and defeat all enemies.

#7: Prayer: In prayer, we show our reliance upon God to act and move. Our entire armor is rooted in His strength. Without God's presence, we are powerless in the fight. We must fight on our knees.

What is your battle plan? How are you going to use the tools that He's given you, so no weapon that's formed against you shall prosper? If you're not preparing, training, or understanding the tools' uses, how will you know which tool to implement? God doesn't just want you to put on the armor of God. He wants you to understand what each component of that armor is, what it does, and why you need it. The strength that comes with this mindset is powerful.

There is a poem called, "The Oak Tree," by Johnny Ray Ryder, Jr. I stumbled across it on a Hallmark card. It's a journey of an oak tree that goes through many seasons that snapped its boughs. It had to face strong winds and heavy rains. It lost all its leaves and was tired of it all until it remembered how far and deep it was rooted in the Earth. At the end of it all, the oak tree realized it was still standing because its roots had stretched so deep down in the earth and grabbed hold and locked into it that soil that even when the strongest winds and the strongest rains came, it was still standing. Sure, it wavered from time to time, but because it had taken its roots and planted them firmly and deeply in the soil, it was rooted in something that could hold it up because it knew the power of being rooted.

When I think back to my journey of finding the discrepancies in my life to my darkest moment of wanting to take my life to God restoring my ability and my desire to live, I said, "God, you're so good to me." As women, we live up to these roles, titles, expectations, and the standards society has placed on us. I got tired of feeling like a failure. I got tired of believing I was not enough. I got tired of feeling like this is all I can do, and this is what my life would be, BUT when I claimed my faith, picked up my cross, and got around like-minded women, I decided to stay and take my stand as a woman. I came to the end of me. When I got tired of being a wounded woman, I became a WARRIOR WOMAN. God is not looking for perfection. He is looking for progression. I encourage you to pick up your cross. Root yourself in faith. Become the woman God desired and designed you to be.

You are more than:

your wounds...

your womb...

your wedding ring...

You are a Warrior!

Epilogue

CAN YOU FEEL THAT shift in you? You may be wondering how you can feel so different after reading this book? It's simple really. You believe it! You believe in the possibility. You believe there is hope! Most of all, you believe in yourself again!

You believe that you can become the woman you desire to be. You believe that your life doesn't have to finish the way it's going or the way it started. Now you know you can be in control of the journey.

You are similar to the woman in Nikki Giovani's poem. She made a decision to become the woman she wanted to be without concern of what others thought she should be. She believed she could, so she did.

Gone are the days of feeling less than, ungrateful, or unfulfilled. You now can look forward with courage, hope, love, and acceptance. Now that you know the possibilities of who you desire to be are endless, you can become her despite the challenges that may come your way.

There is a version of a woman inside you who is ready to come out! Now is her time! Now is your time. She is right there! I know you can feel her tugging at your heart strings.

You can picture the happier days ahead, and you are comfortable in your own skin and your own voice.

Let me ask you, do you have one more day to live a life in which you are not living as who you know you could be? Do you have time for one more day of feeling overwhelmed and unseen or time to keep neglecting yourself? Are you tired of walking around as a worrier,when you could be a WARRIOR?

Here are a few things I want you to take with you as you embark on your Warrior journey:

1. You are more than what others see, but it starts internally with you first.

2. Listen to the feedback. It reveals your blind spots. We can't see everything.

3. Problems that are not handled continue to be problems. Expose them.

4. It's in the darkest moments that you begin to appreciate the light.

5. When you are equipped with words and phrases that clearly and easily define you, you know it. No one can take away what you know.

6. A vision without a strategy remains an illusion. What is your vision for who you want to be?

7.   Accept the truth of who you were, who you are, and
     who you will be. Most importantly, remember whose
     you are.

8.   God can use cracked pots. You are beautifully broken
     and sealed with God's liquid gold.

9.   Warrior in Womanhood. Become her. You owe
     yourself at least that.

Once God showed me the power of being a woman,
it was from that moment on that I never looked back.
Instead, I became a woman. I became a Warrior.

No more sitting by the wayside waiting for life to
happen. Warriors cannot walk in bondage. It's time to
break free from the negative beliefs.

Imagine who you would be if you showed up.

Imagine the light you would become for someone
else's darkness.

Imagine just how Divine your purpose is.

Did you just have a moment? I surely did! Sis, the
world needs YOU to show up!

I hope that by sharing my story, you too will make
a new decision to keep going, rise up, and take ownership
of who you are. I hope that you become inspired and
encouraged to show up and be the woman God has called
you to be. Everything you need, you have right now! You
have your desire to change and take action. It's hard. I

know. If you need help, I'm here! Whether it's coaching or community, you do not have to do this alone. You are now a part of a community of Warrior women who are ready to lock arm and arm with you. I would love to hear from you, support you, and encourage you.

I am a WARRIOR and so are you! Keep pushing. Keep moving forward. Keep standing. Someone out there needs YOUR light. It's time to show up!

To my fellow Warrior Women, the Ezers, and the women of faith, may we know them. May we be them. May we raise them. Amen!

Resources & Information

CORE VALUES EXERCISE ADAPTED FROM TAPROO
(http://www.taproot.com/archives/37771)

1. Determine your core values. From the list below, choose and write down every core value that resonates with you. Do not overthink your selections. As you read through the list, simply write down the words that feel like a core value to you personally. If you think of a value you possess that is not on the list, be sure to write it down as well.

Abundance	Autonomy	Cheerfulness
Acceptance	Balance	Cleverness
Accountability	Being the Best	Community
Achievement	Benevolence	Commitment
Advancement	Boldness	Compassion
Adventure	Brilliance	Cooperation
Advocacy	Calmness	Collaboration
Ambition	Caring	Consistency
Appreciation	Challenge	Contribution
Attractiveness	Charity	Creativity

Credibility	Humility	Personal
Curiosity	Humor	Development
Daring	Inclusiveness	Proactive
Decisiveness	Independence	Professionalism
Dedication	Individuality	Quality
Dependability	Innovation	Recognition
Diversity	Inspiration	Risk Taking
Empathy	Intelligence	Safety
Encouragement	Intuition	Security
Enthusiasm	Joy	Service
Ethics	Kindness	Spirituality
Excellence	Knowledge	Stability
Expressiveness	Leadership	Peace
Fairness	Learning	Perfection
Family	Love	Playfulness
Friendships	Loyalty	Popularity
Flexibility	Making a	Power
Freedom	Difference	Preparedness
Fun	Mindfulness	Proactivity
Generosity	Motivation	Professionalism
Grace	Optimism	Punctuality
Growth	Open-	Recognition
Flexibility	Mindedness	Relationships
Happiness	Originality	Reliability
Health	Passion	Resilience
Honesty	Performance	Resourcefulness

Responsibility   Teamwork   Versatility

Responsiveness   Thankfulness   Vision

Security   Thoughtfulness   Warmth

Self-Control   Traditionalism   Wealth

Selflessness   Trustworthiness   Well-Being

Simplicity   Understanding   Wisdom

Stability   Uniqueness   Zeal

Success   Usefulness

2. Group all similar values together from the list of values you just created. Group them in a way that makes sense to you, personally. Create a maximum of five groupings. If you have more than five groupings, drop those least important. See the example below.

Abundance	Acceptance	Appreciation	Balance	Cheerfulness
Growth	Compassion	Encouragement	Health	Fun
Wealth	Inclusiveness	Thankfulness	Personal	Happiness
Security	Intuition	Thoughtfulness	Development	Humor
Freedom	Kindness	Mindfulness	Spirituality	Inspiration
Independence	Love		Well-being	Joy
Flexibility	Making a			Optimism
Peace	Difference			Playfulness
	Open-			
	Mindedness			
	Trustworthiness			
	Relationships			

3. Choose one word within each grouping that best represents the label for the entire group. Again, do not overthink your labels. There are no right or wrong answers. You are defining the answer that is right for you. See the example below – the label chosen for the grouping is **bolded**.

Abundance	Acceptance	Appreciation	Balance	Cheerfulness
Growth	Compassion	Encouragement	Health	Fun
Wealth	Inclusiveness	Thankfulness	Personal	Happiness
Security	Intuition	Thoughtfulness	Development	Humor
Freedom	Kindness	**Mindfulness**	Spirituality	Inspiration
Independence	Love		**Well-being**	Joy
Flexibility	**Making a**			**Optimism**
Peace	**Difference**			Playfulness
	Open-Mindedness			
	Trustworthiness			
	Relationships			

How Solid is Your Bedrock (Foundation)?

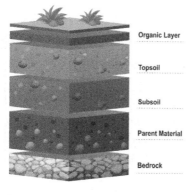

Organic Layer

Topsoil

Subsoil

Parent Material

Bedrock

Your personal foundation are the principles by which you live. Based on the set principles, you develop boundaries, values and beliefs and mindsets. Are you operating based on your principles? Are you consistent in living out your values based on your principles? This worksheet will help expose your principles, values and beliefs and identify how you operate and why.

The table below breaks down who each layer applies to our life. Here you will start to see how each layer affects the one above and below.

Foundation Layer or Word	Definition
Organic Layer **(Society)**	This layer represents what we put out to the world. Often what we truly feel is not congruent with what we put out to the world. You will want to explore how you present yourself based on what you think people want to see. Ex. I am a female and I am supposed to be feminine so I act that way – Girly girl.
Topsoil **(Your past)**	What are some of the ideas or expectations you believed based on your family history, past relationship, work experience, etc. Ex. I am supposed to get married and have children because my parents did. Or I must graduate college.
Subsoil **(Fears &** **Strongholds,** **Offenses)**	This layer is a little more deeply rooted. This is usually the layer that most people stop digging at because they hit a rock but it's not bedrock. They get stuck here in their perceptions. These rocks are considered loose deposits (landfill, debris or junk) that hold space or what could be considered fears, strongholds or Offenses we have experienced. You can change the material fill just like you can change your perspective by digging through this area and removing what's not needed and replacing it with better material.
Parent Material	This area stems from your childhood and upbringing. There may be learned habits, personality traits, family values and beliefs that were instilled, imprinted or impacted at this stage. You were born as you are but this layer serves as your first level of outside influence.

Bedrock	This is the Earth's crust. This is solid rock. It takes a lot, if anything at all, to waiver this final and primary layer of your foundation
Principle	a fundamental truth or proposition that serves as the foundation for a system of belief or behavior or for a *chain of reasoning.*
Offense	Annoyance or resentment brought about by a *perceived* insult to or *disregard* for oneself or *one's standards or principles*
Fears/Stronghold	An unpleasant emotion caused by the belief that someone or something is dangerous, likely to cause pain, or a threat. Strongholds hold onto any beliefs derived from fear deep within our spirit

Surface Layer: What do you present to the outside world? Are you authentically you?

Topsoil: What are some of the ideas or concepts you believe are true based on your past?

Subsoil & Weathered Rock: What are the fears ,strongholds or offenses you have held onto, how do they make you feel and operate?

Bedrock: Based on everything you wrote above, what principles are you operating off of? Where did you get the principle(s) from?

So how SOLID is your Bedrock?

Are you easily moved?

Do you waiver in your principles?

Are your principles rooted in a source other than yourself?

Do you need to change some of your current principles?

Write down your current principles, assess if you are going to keep them or if you need to change them, do some research and write out the new one.

Current Principle	Keep: Yes or No	New Principle
Ex. Whenever I fail I learn valuable lessons that make me smarter and stronger	**YES / NO**	
I alleviate stress by playing and having FUN!	**YES / NO**	
Forgive Frequently	**YES / NO**	
	YES / NO	
	YES / NO	
	YES / NO	
	YES / NO	
	YES / NO	
	YES / NO	

Sermons

Series: *Planted, Not Buried* - Transformation Church, Pastor
Michael Todd
Series: *Relationship Goals Series1 & 2*, Transformation
Church, Pastor Michael Todd
Series: *Forgiveness University*, Transformation Church, Pastor
Michael Todd
Series: *All Strings Attached*, Transformation Church, Pastor
Michael Todd
Series: *The Purpose Paradox*, Transformation Church, Pastor
Michael Todd
Offenses: Pastor Steven Furtick
At the Core - Pastor Sarah Jakes Roberts
Girl, Get Up - Pastor Sarah Jakes Roberts
The Armor - Priscilla Shirer

Books

9 Thoughts that Change My Marriage, Sheila Wray Gregoire
Integrity, Dr. Henry Cloud
Love & Respect, Emerson Eggerichs
7 Habits of Highly Effective People, Steven Covey
BIFF, Quick Responses to High Conflict People, Bill Eddy, LCSW, Esq.
Boundaries, Dr. Henry Cloud and Dr. John Townsend
Boundaries in Marriage, Dr. Henry Cloud and Dr. John Townsend
Safe People, Dr. Henry Cloud and Dr. John Townsend
Woman Evolve, Sarah Jakes Roberts

Community

Facebook: Warrior Womanhood

Coaching: Warrior Academy

Websites:

Self-Therapy Journey, www.selftherapyjourney.com

To Learn More

www.thecapacitycoach.com

Synopsis

You are a Warrior! A Warrior in Womanhood.

I was the one who looked like she had it all. I had the house, the husband, the family, and the good job. I lived up to all my titles and carried out all my roles, but internally, I was struggling. I found myself trapped in the cycle of people-pleasing and performing to be the "best." I had to be the best mom, the best wife, the best daughter, and so on to the point that I looked up one day and wondered where I was. I was tired of operating in and living up to all these titles. I just wanted to find my way back to myself.

Like me, you may be caught up trying to live up to the expectations of others or in the comparison trap known as social media. A part of you feels missing, and you want that back. You want HER back! It was my rock bottom moment that served as my slingshot to go from wounded to Warrior.

In Warrior in Womanhood, you will learn practical tips and tools to help you

- Identify your emotional trauma triggers.
- Learn how to stop the self-sabotage process and replace it with self-love and self-acceptance.
- Root yourself in your identity outside any role or title in which you serve.
- Identify practical tools to create a spiritual battle kit for future use.
- Strengthen your faith walk.

Yes, sis, it's your time. No longer will you shrink. No longer will you walk in fear, shame, guilt, or worry. Who you are is beautiful, and you are worthy of living your best life. It is by design too! You are stronger than you know, braver than you think, and more powerful than you ever could imagine. You are a woman! I love you. I encourage you! I support you! Welcome to Warrior Womanhood!

About the Author

Ayana Henderson has worked and consulted in the human resources field for over 10 years. As an HR professional, life coach, and communication and behavioral consultant, she has learned four things people, specifically women, desire most. The desire to find out who they truly are, what they want, and how to speak up and show up as their authentic selves unapologetically. Ayana knows what it's like to lose and shrink parts of yourself from the journey and trauma that life brings. Drawing from experience over the last two decades as a wife, mother, and personal and professional development specialist, Ayana created Warrior Womanhood. Warrior Womanhood helps women who have also lost parts of themselves, through their own life journey reclaim their voice and their value, so they can go from wounded women to Warrior Women. Ayana lives with her husband and children just north of Atlanta, GA.

Made in the USA
Las Vegas, NV
03 September 2021